MENTAL PERFORMANCE SERIES

ACHIEVING GREATNESS: BUILDING MENTAL TOUGHNESS

Volume 2

COACH P.JIM PUSATERI

Contents

PASSION

THE FIRE THAT STARTS YOUR JOURNEY

CHAPTER 1

Defining Greatness Beyond Talent

"Greatness is not a function of talent alone. It is the result of daily discipline, focused effort, and mental toughness."

Greatness is a word that gets used so often that it has almost lost its weight. We label athletes great, leaders great,
teams great, and moments great. But very rarely do we stop long enough to define what greatness actually is.

If greatness were simply about talent, the world would be overflowing with high achievers. Every locker room, classroom,
and workplace is filled with individuals who have ability. Yet far too many never reach the level they are capable of.
Not because they lack talent — but because talent alone is not enough.

Talent opens doors. Mental toughness keeps them open.

I've coached athletes with natural ability that stood out the moment they stepped on the field. Speed. Strength. Skill.
But I've also watched some of those same athletes disappear when things got hard — when expectations increased, when competition stiffened, or when comfort was removed.

At the same time, I've seen athletes with less natural ability rise to leadership roles, earn trust, and outperform
more gifted teammates. The difference was never talent. The difference was mental toughness.

"Potential without discipline eventually turns into regret."

Talent might earn you an opportunity or a head start. But talent alone will never sustain success. Mental toughness
determines how you respond when progress slows, when adversity hits, and when pressure increases.

One of the most dangerous compliments a person can receive is being told they have "so much potential." Potential sounds
good, but potential without action becomes frustration. At some point, potential stops being encouragement and starts
becoming a reminder of what was never fully realized.

Comfort is one of the greatest enemies of greatness.

Comfort feels good in the moment, but it quietly limits growth. Greatness is built in early mornings, late nights, boring repetitions, uncomfortable conversations, and moments where no one is watching. Mental toughness is choosing discipline over excuses and standards over feelings.

"Greatness is built when no one is clapping."

Greatness is not something you are born with. It is something you choose to pursue daily. That choice shows up in effort,
attitude, preparation, and response. Mentally tough individuals do not wait to feel motivated — they rely on habits,
standards, and structure.

Pressure does not create weaknesses. Pressure reveals them.

Under pressure, habits surface. Preparation shows. Mindset is exposed. Mentally tough people don't rise to the moment —
they fall back on their training. They trust their preparation. They control what they can control.

This is a consistent theme discussed on the Mental Toughness by Coach P Podcast. Over and over again, athletes, coaches,
and performers at every level share the same lesson: when pressure

hits, you don't become something new — you reveal
what you've trained to be.

"Pressure doesn't break you — it introduces you to yourself."

Greatness is doing the right thing when it is hard. It is consistency
over time. It is composure when emotions run high.
It is accountability when excuses would be easier.

Mental toughness is built through daily discipline, intentional habits,
honest self-evaluation, and a willingness to be
uncomfortable. It is not developed overnight. It is earned through
repetition and commitment.

This chapter lays the foundation for Volume 2. The chapters ahead
focus on applying mental toughness under pressure,
developing consistency, and living by higher standards — not just in
sports, but in life.

Reflection Questions:

1. Where have I relied on talent instead of discipline?
2. How do I respond when pressure challenges me?
3. What uncomfortable habits do I need to embrace to pursue
   greatness?

Action Step:

Commit to one discipline-based habit this week — especially on days
when motivation is low. Track it. Finish it.
Build the mental toughness standard.

"Greatness isn't built in comfort. It's built through mental toughness."

www.InspiringThem.com

CHAPTER 2

The Standard You're Willing to Live By

"You don't rise to your goals. You fall to your standards."

"Your life moves in the direction of the standards you tolerate."

There are two versions of you — the one you talk about, and the one your standards reveal.

You may say you want greatness. You may say you want growth, discipline, and consistency.
But your life does not move toward what you say. It moves toward what you tolerate.

The standard you live by — not the goal you announce — determines your direction.

***

Standards Are Internal, Not External

Goals are visible. Standards are invisible.
Goals are exciting. Standards are quiet.
Goals are public. Standards are private.

Your standard shows up in how you speak to yourself, how you respond to correction, how you handle discomfort,
and how you give effort when no one is evaluating you.

"Every time you tolerate something below your potential, you train yourself to accept it."

The Negotiation Voice

There is a voice inside all of us that negotiates.
"Just this once."
"I'll push harder tomorrow."
"I'm tired."

The negotiation voice erodes your standard slowly. You don't wake up undisciplined.
You slowly lower the bar through repeated permission.

Mental toughness is the quiet refusal to negotiate with excuses.

Emotional Standards

What is your emotional standard?
Do you allow frustration to control you?
Do you allow criticism to shake you?
Or do you maintain composure?

"Your emotional maturity sets the ceiling on your performance."

If your mood controls your effort, your performance will always fluctuate.

Thought Standards

The conversation in your head becomes the standard of your confidence.

Do you reinforce belief — or rehearse doubt?

Mental toughness requires disciplined thinking. You cannot perform consistently if your thoughts are inconsistent.

The Slow Drift

Standards rarely collapse dramatically. They drift — quietly, privately.

Skipping the extra rep.
Avoiding hard conversations.
Choosing comfort once.

Repetition builds identity. Identity builds performance.

"What you repeat becomes who you are."

The Standard and Self-Respect

Standards are tied to self-respect.
When you hold yourself to a higher standard, you are telling yourself:
"I am worth discipline."

Lowering your standard repeatedly sends the opposite message.

Mental toughness is self-respect expressed through discipline.

The Internal Thermostat

Everyone has a performance comfort level — a thermostat.

If excellence feels foreign, you will unconsciously return to average.

"If excellence feels foreign, you will unconsciously return to average."

Raise your thermostat. Expand what feels normal.

A Reflective Story: The Almost Athlete

Every coach remembers the "almost" athlete.

Almost great.
Almost consistent.
Almost disciplined.

Flashes of brilliance — but no sustained standard.

They are not incapable. They are inconsistent.

Inconsistency is tied to internal standards.

Sport Application

You can observe an athlete for five minutes and identify their standard.

After mistakes — do they reset or disconnect?
During conditioning — do they finish or fade?
In film — are they engaged or distracted?

"Game day exposes what practice has rehearsed."

The Weight of Private Decisions

No one sees the extra discipline, the refusal to complain, the controlled reaction.
But those decisions compound.

"Your private discipline determines your public performance."

Pressure Tests Alignment

Pressure doesn't create greatness. It tests alignment.

If your internal standard is high, pressure sharpens you.
If it is low, pressure exposes you.

Life Beyond Sport

The standard you build in athletics becomes the foundation for life.

It shapes leadership, career, relationships, and identity.

Greatness is rare — not because ability is rare, but because high standards are rare.

Reflection Questions:

1. What behaviors do I repeatedly tolerate from myself?
2. Where am I drifting privately?
3. What is my emotional response standard?
4. What identity am I reinforcing daily?

Action Step:

Choose one internal standard to raise this week — emotional control, thought discipline, effort consistency, or accountability.

Do not announce it. Live it. Refuse to negotiate it.

You do not become great accidentally.

You become great deliberately — through repeated decisions, quiet discipline, and non-negotiable standards.

Your goals may inspire you.

But your standards will define you.

THE STANDARD OF GREATNESS

CHAPTER 3

Mental Endurance — Mastering the Long Game

Greatness is not built in moments.

It is built in seasons.

It is built in the quiet, repetitive, often unnoticed days where discipline is required long after motivation fades. If Volume 2 is about The Standard of Greatness, then mental endurance is one of its foundational pillars. Because no standard matters if you cannot sustain it.

Anyone can start strong.

Very few can stay strong.

That is where the long game begins.

THE PROBLEM WITH SHORT-TERM THINKING

We live in a world addicted to quick results—quick highlights, quick recognition, quick success. But greatness does not operate on a short-term timeline.

In athletics, championships are not won in one game. They are built through months of conditioning, film study, repetition, recovery, and relentless attention to detail. In the classroom, mastery is built through daily focus. In life, meaningful success is compounded over time.

Short-term thinking asks: "How fast can I win?"

Long-term thinking asks: "How long can I stay committed?"

Mental endurance is the ability to stay committed when progress feels slow. It is the discipline to remain focused when excitement fades. The middle is where most people quit.

THE MIDDLE IS WHERE GREATNESS IS BUILT

The beginning is exciting. The finish line is rewarding. But the middle reveals character.

The middle is early mornings when no one is watching. Extra reps when no one is filming. Studying when no one is checking.

Talent may start the journey.

Mental endurance sustains it.

Story Layer 1: The Offseason Athlete

Consider the athlete who doesn't start as a freshman. He could quit. He could complain. Or he could endure. He lifts when others sleep. He studies film when others scroll. By senior year, he isn't just talented—he's seasoned. Endurance turned potential into performance.

Story Layer 2: The Slow Academic Climb

The student who struggles early could label themselves incapable. Instead, they commit to steady improvement—one assignment at a time. Months later, grades improve. Confidence grows. Not because of a breakthrough moment—but because of consistent effort.

Story Layer 3: The Long Career Path

The professional who doesn't get promoted immediately must choose: bitterness or growth. Those who endure use seasons of waiting to build skill and leadership. When opportunity arrives, they are ready—not lucky.

DISCIPLINE OVER EMOTION

Mental endurance is disciplined, not emotional.

Emotion says, "Take today off."

Endurance says, "Stay the course."

Standards are commitments independent of mood. When you operate from standards instead of feelings, you create stability.

THE LONG GAME IN SPORTS

Everyone wants the spotlight. Few embrace development.

Mental endurance in sports means showing up when second string. Competing when tired. Remaining coachable when corrected. Preparing like a starter before you are one.

That is endurance.

THE LONG GAME IN LIFE

Careers, leadership, confidence—all are built through consistent deposits.

In our newest release, Mental Performance Series Volume 1: Passion, Belief, Achievement, we discuss how passion starts the fire, belief sustains it, and achievement becomes the byproduct of disciplined consistency.

Passion begins the journey.

Belief fuels it.

Endurance finishes it.

THREE KEYS TO MASTERING THE LONG GAME

1. Focus on Daily Deposits

   Win today. Stack disciplined days together.

2. Protect Your Standards

   Standards anchor you when emotions fluctuate.

3. Finish What You Start

   Starting is exciting. Finishing requires endurance.

THE STANDARD OF ENDURANCE

Greatness is built in repetition.

Built in quiet discipline.

Built in unwavering commitment.

Talent opens doors.

Endurance keeps them open.

Master the long game.

Stay disciplined.

Stay steady.

Stay committed.

That is The Standard of Greatness.

— Coach P

CHAPTER 4

Composure – The Discipline of Emotional Control

"Emotional control is not weakness. It is power under discipline."

Composure is misunderstood. Some think it means you don't care. Others think it means you suppress emotion. But composure is not the absence of emotion — it is control of response.

Anyone can stay calm when winning. The separator appears when pressure rises, when mistakes happen, when expectations tighten, and when momentum shifts.

Emotions are human. Frustration, disappointment, anger, pressure - they are natural. Mental toughness does not eliminate emotion. It disciplines response.

Emotion is automatic. Response is intentional.

Between stimulus and response there is a gap. Most collapse it and react immediately. Elite performers expand it. They feel the emotion, but they choose their behavior.

Mistakes do not destroy performance. Emotional reactions do.

In sport, emotional instability is expensive. Body language drops. Communication weakens. Focus narrows. Leadership erodes. One uncontrolled reaction can shift momentum.

Composure spreads. So does chaos.

Your composure becomes someone else's courage.

Internally, composure begins with interpretation. The event is neutral. The meaning you assign creates the emotion. Change the meaning, and you change the response.

"The meaning you assign determines the emotion you experience."

Ego threatens composure. Ego wants to protect image. Humility strengthens composure. Stable identity reduces reactive emotion.

Story Reflection:

Late in a game, a critical shot was missed. In that moment, two futures existed: one driven by frustration, the other by recovery and leadership. The difference was not talent — it was emotional discipline.

Composure is revealed when disappointment arrives.

Emotion transfers. Energy spreads. You are never managing only yourself — you are influencing everyone around you.

Calm body. Clear mind.

Physiological regulation matters. Slow breathing steadies heart rate. Posture influences confidence. Nervous system control precedes mental clarity.

Delay reaction. Pause. Breathe. Choose.

Most emotional damage occurs in immediate response. Delayed reaction builds maturity.

In the fourth quarter, fatigue rises and pressure intensifies. The composed athlete communicates clearly and stays steady. The unstable athlete forces, blames, and disconnects.

Recovery speed separates competitors.

Mistake → Reset → Re-engage.

Outside sport, composure builds trust. In conflict, criticism, or stress, regulated response strengthens influence.

Emotional control is maturity under pressure.

Reflection Questions:

1. How do I respond after mistakes?
2. Does my emotional reaction help or hurt those around me?
3. What reset phrase will I use in pressure moments?
4. Where in life must I practice stronger emotional discipline?

Action Step:

For the next week, practice a three-step reset:

1. Slow breath.
2. Neutral posture.
3. Short command phrase.

Train the gap between stimulus and response.

You cannot control every moment. But you can control your response.

Greatness does not belong to the most emotional. It belongs to the most controlled.

Emotional control is power under discipline.

www.InspiringThem.com

CHAPTER 5

Identity Over Outcome
Who You Become Matters More Than What You Win

n sports and in life, we live in a world that is obsessed with outcomes.

Scoreboards.
Statistics.
Championship rings.
Job titles.
Social media highlights.

We measure success by the result.

Did you win?
Did you get the promotion?
Did you reach the goal?

But the truth about greatness is this:

The greatest performers in the world don't chase outcomes.
They build identities.

They decide who they are first.

And once identity is established, the outcomes start to follow.

Today we're going to talk about one of the most powerful principles in mental performance:

Identity Over Outcome.

Because when you build the right identity, success stops being something you chase...
It becomes something you naturally produce.

The Outcome Trap

Many athletes fall into what I call the outcome trap.

They measure themselves by the result.

If they win — they feel confident.
If they lose — they question everything.

But that mindset creates emotional instability.

Your confidence becomes tied to the scoreboard.

And the scoreboard is something you cannot always control.

You can play the best game of your life and still lose.
You can do everything right and still come up short.

That's why elite performers learn a different mental framework.

Instead of asking:
"Did I win?"

They ask:
"Did I live my identity today?"

Because outcomes fluctuate.
But identity is stable.

The Power of Identity

Identity answers a powerful question:
Who am I becoming?

Not just:
What am I achieving?

When athletes operate from identity, their behaviors change.

They don't say:
"I hope I work hard today."

They say:
"I am a hard worker."

They don't say:
"I need to stay disciplined."

They say:
"Discipline is who I am."

And once something becomes part of your identity…
You stop negotiating with it.
You stop debating it.
You simply live it.

Identity in Athletics

The best teams have a very clear identity.
Not just strategy.
Identity.

They know who they are.
They know what they stand for.

At Central High School Football, we talk about our ABC Standards:
Academics
Behavior
Commitment

Those aren't just rules.
They represent the identity of our program.

A Central Bear understands something important.
You don't just play football here.
You represent something bigger.

You represent discipline.
You represent accountability.
You represent doing your part.

Identity Creates Consistency

Outcomes fluctuate.
Identity stabilizes performance.

If your identity is:
"I win when things go well."

Then when adversity hits…
You struggle.

But if your identity is:
"I am someone who fights through adversity."

Then when difficulty shows up…
You expect it.
You are prepared for it.

And that changes how you respond.

The Story of the Weight Room

There are two types of athletes.

The first athlete lifts when they feel like it.
When motivation is high.
When someone is watching.

The second athlete operates from identity.

Their identity says:
"I am someone who prepares."
"I am someone who gets better every day."
"I am someone who outworks yesterday."

So they show up even when it's inconvenient.
Even when nobody is watching.

Because preparation is part of who they are.

Identity Shapes Behavior

People act in alignment with who they believe they are.

If someone believes they are lazy...
Their behavior supports that belief.

If someone believes they are disciplined...
Their behavior supports that belief.

This is why identity is so powerful.
It sits at the root of behavior.

If you want to change your results...
Start with identity.

Building the Identity of Greatness

Define the characteristics of the person you want to become.

For athletes this might include:
Discipline
Resilience
Accountability
Consistency
Preparation
Team-first mindset

At our program we often say:
"Do Your Part."

That phrase represents identity.

Teams don't become great through talent alone.
They become great through identity.

The Long Game

Outcomes happen in moments.
Identity is built over time.

A game lasts four quarters.
A season lasts a few months.

But identity lasts a lifetime.

The habits you build through sports follow you into life.

Discipline becomes career success.
Commitment becomes leadership.
Resilience becomes the ability to move forward through adversity.

Identity vs External Validation

Many athletes chase external validation.
Likes.
Followers.
Recognition.

But external validation is temporary.
Identity is internal.

When your identity is strong...
You show up and do the work.

The Standard You Live By

What standard do you live by?

Not when it's easy.
Not when people are watching.

But when nobody is around.

Your standard defines your identity.
Your identity defines your habits.
Your habits define your future.

The Identity Decision

Identity is a decision.

It's something you build every day through choices and discipline.

You become the person your habits support.

Reflection

What identity are your daily habits reinforcing?
Are your actions aligned with the person you want to become?
Are you chasing outcomes or building identity?

Closing Message

The scoreboard tells part of the story.
But the deeper story is about identity.

Who did you become through the process?

Greatness is not built in moments of victory.
Greatness is built in daily identity.

So don't just chase outcomes.
Build an identity.

Because when identity is strong...
Success becomes a byproduct.

Coach P
Train your mind. Inspire others. Achieve greatness.

www.InspiringThem.com

CHAPTER 6

The Inner Voice Advantage
Mastering the Conversation Inside Your Mind

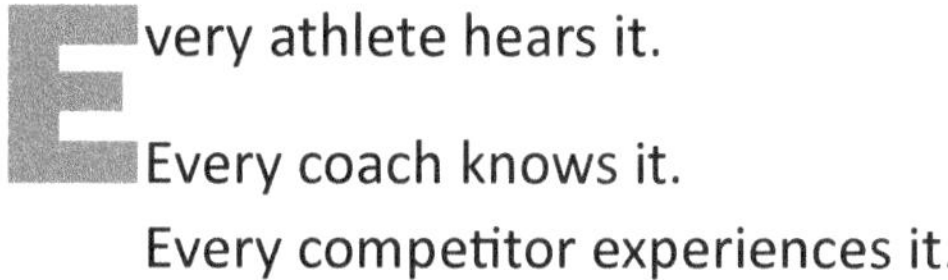

Every athlete hears it.

Every coach knows it.

Every competitor experiences it.

That voice inside your head.

Sometimes it builds you up.
Sometimes it tears you down.
Sometimes it pushes you forward.
Sometimes it tries to hold you back.

But here is one of the most important truths about performance:

The most important voice you will ever hear is the one inside your own mind.

Not the crowd.
Not your coach.
Not your critics.
Not social media.

Your inner voice.

And the athletes who learn to control that voice gain a powerful edge over the competition.

I call it the Inner Voice Advantage.

Because the difference between average performers and elite performers often comes down to this:

How they talk to themselves under pressure.

The Silent Game Inside Your Mind

Most people think competition happens on the field.

But the truth is the biggest competition happens inside your mind.

It happens when things go wrong.
It happens after mistakes.
It happens when pressure rises.

That's when your inner voice starts talking.

You might hear things like:

"I can't mess this up."
"What if I fail?"
"Everyone is watching."
"I'm not ready for this."

Those thoughts influence your body, confidence, decisions, and performance.

If you don't learn to manage that voice, it will manage you.

The Power of Self-Talk

Sports psychology has shown that your brain listens to the words you repeat.

When your self-talk is negative, confidence drops and focus disappears.

When your self-talk is strong and intentional, your mind stabilizes and performance improves.

Elite athletes don't eliminate pressure.

They learn to control the conversation inside their mind.

The Moment After the Mistake

Every athlete makes mistakes.

Quarterbacks throw interceptions.
Receivers drop passes.
Linemen miss blocks.
Defenders miss tackles.

Mistakes are part of competition.

But the real difference happens in the 10 seconds after the mistake.

Some athletes say:
"That was terrible."
"I always mess up."

Elite athletes say:
"Next play."
"Reset."
"I've got this."

They move forward quickly, and that ability separates good players from great competitors.

The Confidence Builder

Confidence is not something you wait for.

Confidence is built through preparation and self-talk.

Elite athletes remind themselves:

"I'm ready."
"I've prepared for this."
"I belong here."

That voice creates calm in the middle of chaos.

The Weight Room Voice

Every athlete knows the moment when the weight feels heavy and fatigue sets in.

Your inner voice starts negotiating.

"That's enough for today."
"You've already done enough."

But disciplined athletes respond with:

"One more."
"Finish the rep."
"Get better today."

Those small moments of discipline build mental toughness.

Replacing the Negative Voice

You cannot eliminate negative thoughts entirely.

But you can replace them.

Instead of:
"I can't do this."

Say:
"I'm prepared for this."

Instead of:
"I messed up."

Say:
"Next play."

Instead of:
"This is too hard."

Say:
"This is where I grow."

The goal is intentional thinking.

Identity and Inner Voice

Your inner voice is tied to your identity.

If your identity says you quit when things get hard, your inner voice will support that.

But if your identity says:

"I am resilient."
"I am disciplined."
"I move forward."

Your inner voice reinforces that strength.

The Reset Routine

Elite athletes develop reset routines.

First — Breathe.

Second — Reset the thought:
"Next play."

Third — Refocus on the task.
Reset routines prevent one mistake from becoming two.

Training the Inner Voice
Mental strength is built through repetition.

Habits like positive self-talk during workouts, encouraging teammates, and reminding yourself of your standards train your inner voice.

Over time it becomes stronger, calmer, and more confident.

The Competitive Advantage

At high levels of competition everyone is talented.

Everyone is strong.

Everyone is fast.

The difference becomes mental.

Athletes who master their inner voice gain a powerful advantage because their mind stays steady under pressure.

Reflection

What does your inner voice sound like during competition?

Does it build confidence or create doubt?

Does it move you forward or hold you back?

Are you intentionally training that voice?

Closing Message

Every athlete trains their body.

They lift weights.
They run.
They practice.
They watch film.

But the greatest performers train their mind as well.

They train their thoughts.
They train their self-talk.
They train their response to adversity.

Because when pressure shows up, your inner voice becomes your coach.

And when that voice is strong, calm, and confident, you gain the Inner Voice Advantage.

Coach P
Train your mind. Inspire others. Achieve greatness.

CHAPTER 7

Clarity Under Pressure
The Discipline to Think Clearly When It Matters Most

The Moment That Speeds Everything Up

Pressure has a way of changing everything. The clock feels faster. The noise gets louder. The moment feels bigger. And what once felt simple suddenly feels overwhelming. This is the reality of pressure—it doesn't just challenge your ability, it challenges your thinking.

Most people believe pressure is what causes mistakes. But that's not the truth. Pressure simply reveals what is already there. It exposes your habits, your preparation, and most importantly—your mindset.

When the moment speeds up, your mind wants to speed up with it. That's where mistakes happen. That's where confusion creeps in. That's where performance breaks down.

But elite performers do something different. They slow the moment down. They simplify. They focus.

Pressure doesn't create confusion. It exposes it. And in that moment, clarity becomes your greatest advantage.

The Principle: Clarity Creates Control

Clarity is what allows you to stay in control when everything around you feels out of control.

It means knowing exactly what matters and eliminating everything that doesn't. It means locking into your role, your responsibility, and your execution.

Clarity removes hesitation. It builds confidence. It creates consistency.

When your mind is clear, your actions become decisive. You don't second-guess. You don't hesitate. You simply execute.

And that's the difference between average and elite.

Athlete Layer: The 4th Quarter Drive

It's the 4th quarter. Two minutes left. The game is on the line.

The crowd is loud. The energy is high. Every player feels the pressure.

And in that moment, most athletes start thinking about everything except what matters.

They think about the outcome. They think about the consequences. They think about what happens if they fail.

But the athletes who perform at a high level don't do that.

They simplify the moment.

The quarterback focuses on his read. The lineman focuses on his block. The receiver focuses on his route.

At Central, we say: Do Your Part.

That is clarity under pressure. That is discipline in action.

No one tries to do everything. Everyone does something with precision.

That's how you win.

Life Layer: When Pressure Feels Personal

Pressure doesn't stay on the field. It follows you into life.

It shows up in your decisions. It shows up in your responsibilities. It shows up in moments where the outcome matters.

And just like in sports, most people struggle because they lose clarity.

They overthink. They hesitate. They allow fear to control their actions.

They start focusing on everything that could go wrong instead of focusing on what they can control.

Clarity in life is about simplifying the moment.

What is the next step?

That question brings focus. That question creates movement. That question eliminates overwhelm.

You don't need to have everything figured out. You just need to know your next move.

And then take it.

Business Layer: Leadership Under Pressure

In business, pressure comes in the form of decisions, deadlines, and expectations.

And when pressure rises, leadership is tested.

Leaders who lack clarity react emotionally. They rush decisions. They create confusion.

But strong leaders bring clarity to chaos.

They slow the situation down. They identify what matters. They make clear, confident decisions.

And when they do that, others follow.

Clarity builds trust. Clarity builds confidence. Clarity builds results.

Because when everything feels uncertain, people look for direction.

And direction comes from clarity.

The Clarity Execution Model

When pressure hits, don't rely on emotion. Rely on structure.

Identify your role. What is your responsibility in this moment?

Eliminate the noise. What distractions can you remove?

Control your body. Slow your breathing. Stay composed.

Trust your preparation. You have done the work.

Execute. Take action with confidence and purpose.

This model is simple, but powerful. It allows you to stay focused when others lose control.

The Enemy: Emotional Noise

Fear. Doubt. Anxiety. Pressure from others. Pressure from within.

All of it creates noise.

And that noise clouds your thinking. It pulls your focus away from what matters. It causes hesitation.

Mental toughness is not about eliminating the noise. It is about controlling your response to it.

You will feel pressure. You will feel doubt. But you do not have to follow those thoughts.

You can choose clarity.

And that choice changes everything.

Reflection

Where do you lose clarity in your life?

What situations cause you to overthink?

Do you speed up when pressure hits, or do you slow down?

What is one area of your life where you can simplify your thinking right now?

Clarity is not something you find. It is something you build.

Words of Encouragement

When the moment speeds up, slow your mind down.

When the pressure rises, focus on your role.

When doubt creeps in, trust your preparation.

You are more ready than you think.

You are more capable than you realize.

Stay clear. Stay focused. Execute.

Coach P Closing

Built for the Climb.

That means you are built for pressure. You are built for adversity. You are built for the moments that challenge you.

So when that moment comes, don't panic.

Slow it down. Lock it in. Do your part.

Because greatness is built under pressure.

CHAPTER 8

The Power of the Reset
The Discipline to Refocus, Regain Control, and Move Forward

The Moment You Want Back

We've all had that moment. The mistake. The missed opportunity. The play you wish you could do over.

And in that moment, your mind starts racing. You replay it. You question it. You let it sit with you longer than it should.

That's where most people lose control—not because of the mistake itself, but because they stay stuck in it.

The truth is simple. The moment is over. But your response to it is just beginning.

Pressure doesn't just test your ability. It tests your ability to move forward.

And if you can't reset, you can't perform.

The Principle: Reset Creates Response

A reset is not about pretending the mistake didn't happen. It's about choosing what happens next.

You cannot control the last play. You cannot change the last decision. But you can control your focus, your mindset, and your next action.

That's where power lives.

Most people lose twice. First in the mistake. Then in their response.

But disciplined performers understand something different.

They reset quickly. They refocus immediately. They move forward with purpose.

You don't lose because of the mistake. You lose because you never reset.

Athlete Layer: Next Play Mentality

You throw an interception. You miss a tackle. You drop a pass.

Now what?

That question determines everything.

Most athletes carry the mistake into the next play. You can see it in their body language. Their energy drops. Their confidence dips. Their focus disappears.

And now one mistake becomes two. Then three.

But elite athletes have a different mindset.

At Central, we say: Next Play.

Not later. Not eventually. Immediately.

They line back up. They lock back in. They execute again.

They don't forget the mistake. They learn from it.
But they don't carry it.

That is discipline. That is mental toughness.

Great athletes don't eliminate mistakes. They eliminate the time between mistakes and recovery.

Story Layer: The Turning Point

There was a game where everything started going wrong early. Penalties, missed assignments, turnovers.

The momentum shifted quickly.

Some players started pressing. Trying to fix everything at once. Playing outside their role.

But others stayed composed.

They reset.

One play at a time. One drive at a time. One moment at a time.

They didn't try to win the game all at once. They just focused on doing their part.

And slowly, the game changed.

Momentum didn't shift because of one big play. It shifted because of consistent resets.

That's the power of discipline.

Life Layer: Letting Go to Move Forward

Resetting isn't just for sports. It's for life.
You make a mistake. You have a bad day. Things don't go your way.
And instead of moving forward, most people stay stuck.

They replay the situation. They think about what they should have
done. They let one moment affect everything that follows.
But progress in life requires the ability to move forward.
Not perfectly. Not without mistakes. But consistently.

Clarity in life comes from asking one question.
What is my next step?
That question removes overwhelm. That question creates action.

You don't need the full plan. You just need the next move.

Business Layer: Leadership Under Pressure

In business and leadership, mistakes are part of the process.

Decisions won't always work. Plans won't always succeed.
And when those moments happen, leaders are tested.

Weak leaders carry the mistake. They hesitate. They lose clarity.

Strong leaders reset.

They evaluate what happened. They make adjustments. They
communicate clearly. And they move forward.

Because leadership is not about avoiding mistakes.
It's about responding to them.

Teams don't need perfect leaders. They need steady leaders.
And steadiness comes from the ability to reset.

The Reset Framework
When things go wrong, rely on structure.

Recognize it. Acknowledge the mistake without emotion.
Evaluate it. Understand what happened and what needs to change.

Separate from it. That moment does not define you.

Engage the next action. Focus on what is in front of you.
Trust yourself. Move forward with confidence.

This is not complicated. But it requires discipline.
And discipline creates consistency.

The Enemy: Carrying the Moment

The biggest mistake people make is not the mistake itself.

It is carrying it.
They bring frustration, doubt, and hesitation into the next moment.

And now their performance drops, not because of ability, but because of mindset.
You cannot move forward if your mind is stuck in the past.

Carrying the mistake is worse than the mistake itself.

Application: Daily Reset Habits

Resetting is not just for big moments.

It is a daily habit.

Bad rep in practice. Reset.
Bad class. Reset.
Bad meeting. Reset.
Bad decision. Reset.

The more you practice resetting, the faster you recover.
The faster you recover, the stronger you become.

Reflection

Where do you hold onto mistakes?
What situations cause you to lose focus?
Do you reset quickly or carry it with you?
What is one area of your life where you need to reset right now?
Awareness leads to action.
Words of Encouragement
You are going to make mistakes.
You are going to face adversity.
You are going to have moments you wish you could take back.
That is part of the process.
But you are not defined by those moments.
You are defined by your response.

Reset. Refocus. Move forward.

Coach P Closing

Built for the Climb.

That means you are built for pressure. Built for adversity. Built for growth.
So when things don't go your way, don't stay there.

Reset.
Lock back in.
Do your part.

Because success is built on how quickly you respond, not how perfectly you perform.
Take the Next Step

If this message connects with you, take the next step in your mental performance training.

Visit www.Inspiringthem.com

Explore our books, courses, and podcast designed to help you perform under pressure, build confidence, and move forward with purpose.

This is not motivation.
This is training for your mind.

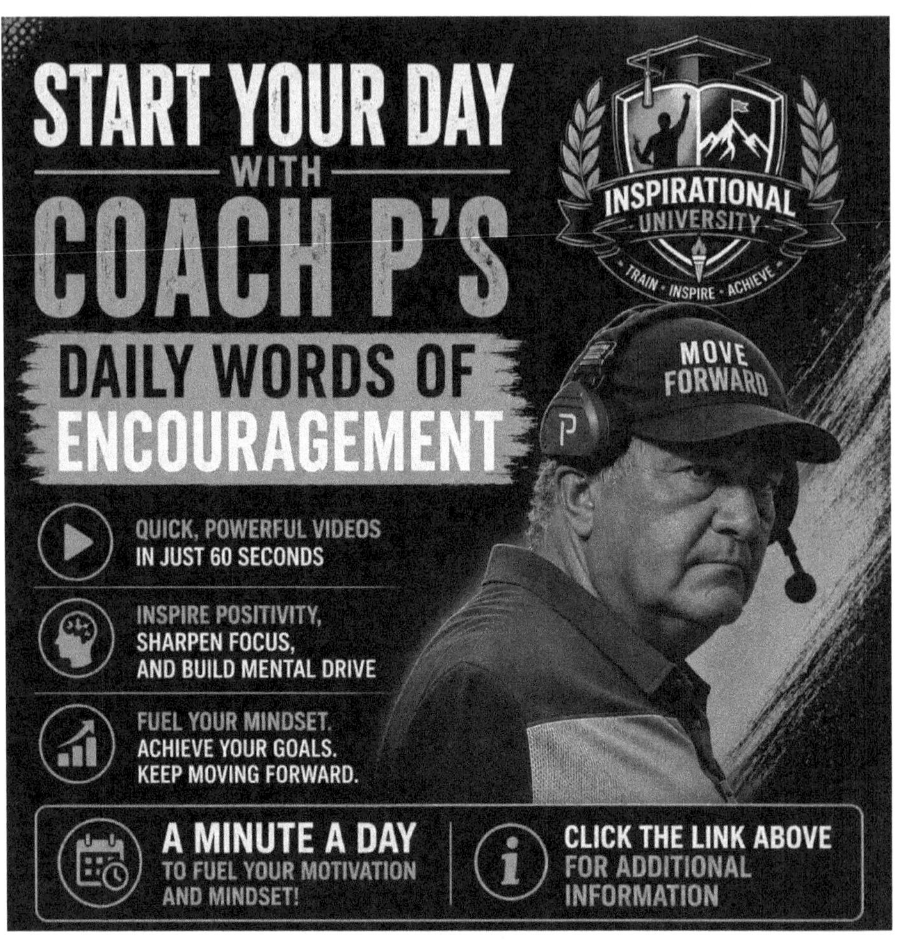

www.InspiringThem.com

CHAPTER 9

Becoming Unshakable

Let me ask you something…

What happens when everything around you starts to fall apart?

When the game isn't going your way…
When life hits you from every angle…
When doubt creeps in…
When pressure builds…

Do you fold?

…or do you stand?

Because today, we're talking about something different.

We're talking about becoming **unshakeable**.

Not perfect.
Not undefeated.
Not untouched.

But unshakeable.

This is the next level of mental performance.
This is what separates average from elite.

And if you can build this…
Nobody can take it from you.

WHAT DOES "UNSHAKEABLE" MEAN?

Being unshakeable doesn't mean nothing affects you.

It means **nothing controls you.**

You still feel pressure…
You still feel doubt…
You still face adversity…

But you don't break.

You don't lose who you are.

🏈 ATHLETE SIDE

You drop a pass…
You throw an interception…
You miss a block…

What happens next?

Most athletes spiral.

Unshakeable athletes?
They reset instantly.

They don't carry the last play into the next one.

💼 LIFE & BUSINESS SIDE

You lose a job.
A deal falls through.
A relationship struggles.

Most people panic…
They lose direction…
They lose belief…

Unshakeable people?

They adjust… but they don't collapse.

☞ That's the difference.

WHY MOST PEOPLE BREAK

Let's be honest…

Most people are fragile.

Not physically…

Mentally.

And here's why:

1. Their identity is tied to outcomes

"If I win, I'm good."
"If I fail, I'm nothing."

That's dangerous.

2. They haven't trained their mind

You train your body…
You train your skills…

But you don't train your thoughts?

That's a problem.

3. They rely on motivation

Motivation is inconsistent.

Mental toughness is not.

This is exactly why I wrote **Mental Toughness by Coach P**.

Because people don't need more hype…

They need a system.

They need tools.

They need training.

👉 And that's also why we built the **Mental Performance Series – Volume 1**.

Because becoming unshakeable isn't luck…

It's built.

THE 4 PILLARS OF BECOMING UNSHAKEABLE

If you want to become unshakeable…

You need structure.

Here it is.

1. CONTROL YOUR INNER VOICE

Everything starts here.

Your self-talk will either build you…

Or break you.

🏈 Athlete:

"I missed that play… I suck."

vs

"Next play. I got this."

💼 Life:

"I failed… I'm done."

VS

"I learned… I adjust… I move forward."

👉 This is what we teach in our **Mindset course: Moving Forward Under Pressure**.

Because if you can control your mind…

You can control your response.

2. DETACH FROM OUTCOMES

You don't control results.

You control effort.
You control preparation.
You control response.

Unshakeable people focus on:

- ✓ The process
- ✓ The standard
- ✓ The next step

3. MASTER THE RESET

You're going to get hit.

That's life.

But how fast do you reset?

🏈 Locker Room Truth:

The best players aren't perfect…

They recover faster than everyone else.

💼 Life Truth:

The most successful people aren't flawless…

They just don't stay down.

☞ Reset is a skill. Train it.

4. BUILD YOUR STANDARD

Standards don't change based on feelings.

Unshakeable people don't say:

"I'll show up when I feel like it."

They say:

"This is who I am. Every day."

That's discipline.

That's identity.

That's power.

LOCKER ROOM STORY

I remember a game...

Everything that could go wrong... did.

Turnovers. Penalties. Mistakes.

You could feel it...
The sideline starting to crack.

Except for one player.

Didn't flinch.
Didn't panic.
Didn't change.

Same voice. Same energy. Same belief.

And guess what?

That steadiness…

Started spreading.

That's what unshakeable looks like.

It's contagious.

LIFE APPLICATION

This isn't just about sports.

This is about life.

When your family is counting on you…
When your career is on the line…
When things don't go your way…

Who are you?

Are you emotional?

Or are you steady?

☞ Because people don't follow talent.

They follow stability.

They trust consistency.

They believe in people who don't break under pressure.

RESOURCES + PROMOTION

If this message is hitting you right now…

That means you're ready to grow.

Here's how you take the next step:

☞ **Book 1:** *Mental Toughness by Coach P*
Build your foundation. Learn how to handle pressure and move forward.

☞ **Book 2:** *Mental Performance Series – Volume 1: Passion, Belief, Achievement*
12 powerful lessons to build your mindset and habits.

☞ **Courses – The Success Bundle:**

• Passion: Find Your Dream Job
• Goal Setting: Achieve All Your Dreams
• Mindset: Move Forward Under Pressure

All designed to help you take control of your life.

☞ **FREE Booklet: The Power of the Inner Game**

This is your starting point.

Because mental performance is the hidden edge.

☞ Get everything at:
InspiringThem.com

THE UNSHAKEABLE STANDARD

Let me leave you with this…

Life is going to test you.

Pressure will find you.
Adversity will hit you.
Doubt will show up.

The question is not if…

The question is:

Will you break… or will you stand?

Because becoming unshakeable…

Isn't about avoiding the storm.

It's about becoming the person…

Who can stand in it.

No matter what.

POWER LINE

Mental Toughness is the ability to…
MOVE FORWARD under pressure.

And unshakeable people?

They don't stop moving.

www.InspiringThem.com

CHAPTER 10

Trusting Your Preparation
The Standard of Greatness

Let me ask you something...

Have you ever walked into a moment and felt completely unsure of yourself?

Your heart is racing...
Your mind is spinning...
And deep down, you're asking yourself one question:

"Am I ready for this?"

Now let me flip it...

Have you ever walked into a moment and felt calm, focused, locked in?

Same situation. Same pressure.

But this time, something is different.

There's no panic.
There's no hesitation.

There's just belief.

That difference is not talent.

It's not luck.
It's not even experience.

It's this:

Preparation.

And more importantly…

Do you trust it?

Because here's the truth most people don't want to hear:

When pressure hits, you don't rise to the level of your expectations.

You fall to the level of your preparation.

Welcome to the Mental Toughness by Coach P Podcast, where we train the mind to move forward under pressure.

This is Chapter 10:

Trusting Your Preparation.

PRESSURE REVEALS, IT DOESN'T CREATE

Pressure is one of the most misunderstood concepts in performance.

People say, "I just couldn't handle the pressure."

No.

The pressure didn't beat you.
It revealed you.

Pressure doesn't create fear.
It exposes uncertainty.

Pressure doesn't create doubt.
It reveals a lack of belief.

Pressure doesn't break you.
It shows you where you're not prepared.

I remember being in a locker room before a big game.

You could feel it.

Some players were loud, joking, loose.

Others were quiet, tense, locked in their own head.

Same team.
Same game.
Same preparation schedule.

But completely different mental states.

Why?

Because one group prepared to play.

The other group prepared to perform under pressure.

There's a difference between being ready and being ready when it matters.

This shows up everywhere in life.

You prepare for a job interview—but do you prepare for the pressure of the interview?

You prepare a speech—but do you prepare for the nerves?

You build a business—but do you prepare for adversity?

Most people prepare for the task.

Very few prepare for the moment.

CONFIDENCE IS EARNED

Let's talk about confidence the right way.

Because confidence is not something you turn on.

Confidence is something you build.

Through repetition.
Through discipline.
Through showing up on the days you do not feel like it.
Through handling the ordinary work with extraordinary consistency.

There are levels to confidence.

The first is fake confidence.

That is all energy, all talk, all surface.

It looks strong until pressure exposes it.

The second is situational confidence.

That says, "I feel good when things are going well."

But when adversity shows up, it disappears.

The third is earned confidence.

This is elite confidence.

It is built through preparation.
Built through repetition.
Built through the discipline of doing the work long before the spotlight arrives.

Confidence is not a feeling.

It is a result of the work you have put in.

Think about a free throw shooter who has shot ten thousand free throws.

That moment at the line does not feel new.

It feels familiar.

Now think about somebody who practiced casually and now wants to trust themselves in a big moment.

That moment feels bigger than them.

The same thing happens in life.

You walk into a meeting, a presentation, a leadership opportunity, or a hard conversation.

If you prepared, studied, rehearsed, and worked, you feel steady.

If you did not, you feel like you are hoping.

Preparation replaces anxiety with belief.

THE PREPARATION GAP

Here is where most people lose.

They confuse activity with preparation.

Being busy is not the same as being prepared.

Showing up is not the same as getting better.

Doing reps is not the same as intentional work.

There are three levels.

Level one is participation.

You show up.
You go through the drills.
You check the box.
You do just enough to say you were there.

That mindset is survival.

Level two is execution.

You focus.
You compete.
You improve.
You care about doing things the right way.

That mindset is performance.

Level three is ownership.

This is where greatness lives.

You prepare with intention.
You train for pressure.
You visualize adversity.
You push beyond comfort.
You own the details.
You do not wait on a coach, a boss, or a circumstance to demand
more from you.

You demand more from yourself.

That mindset is mastery.

Greatness lives in the details you choose not to skip.

So ask yourself this:

Are you preparing to get through it, or preparing to dominate it?

TRUST IS BUILT IN THE DARK

Trust does not happen on game day.

Trust is built in the unseen hours.

Early mornings.
Late nights.
Extra reps.
Extra film.
Extra thought.
Extra discipline.

That is where belief is built.

Not in front of the crowd.

In silence.

The athlete who trusts his preparation is usually the athlete who
stayed after practice.
Watched a little more film.
Took correction seriously.
Worked on weaknesses instead of hiding from them.

The same thing happens in life and business.

The professional who trusts themselves in the room is often the one
who prepared when nobody asked them to.

The leader who stays calm in crisis is often the one who built habits
long before the crisis arrived.

The speaker who looks composed is often the one who rehearsed more than anyone realizes.

What you do in private shows up in public.

That is why private discipline creates public confidence.

THE INNER VOICE

When pressure hits, your inner voice gets louder.

And usually one of two voices shows up.

Voice number one is doubt.

"What if you fail?"
"You are not ready."

"Do not mess this up."

Voice number two is belief.

"You have done this."
"Trust your work."
"Stay calm and execute."

Here is the truth:

You do not choose that voice in the moment.

You train it beforehand.

Your preparation programs your mindset.

If you cut corners, your mind remembers.

If you avoided hard work, your mind knows.

If you prepared with purpose, your mind knows that too.

That is why mental toughness is not just about talking better to yourself.

It is about giving yourself a real reason to believe.

If you want a stronger inner voice, do not just work harder.

Prepare better.

VISUALIZATION

The elite do not only prepare physically.

They prepare mentally.

Visualization is one of the most overlooked tools in performance.

Before the moment arrives, they see the moment.

They feel the pressure.
They rehearse the response.
They imagine themselves calm, steady, and locked in.

If your mind has been there before, your body is more likely to follow.

A quarterback can visualize the read.

A receiver can visualize the catch.
A point guard can visualize making the right play.
A business leader can visualize the hard conversation.
A speaker can visualize controlling the room.
A coach can visualize making a critical adjustment under pressure.

If you can see it clearly, you can perform it more confidently.

This is not pretending.

This is preparation.

You are training your mind to become familiar with the moment before the moment arrives.

WHEN ADVERSITY HITS

Let's be honest.

Preparation does not guarantee perfection.

Things will still go wrong.

Mistakes will still happen.
Passes will still be dropped.
Calls will still be missed.
Plans will still break.
Setbacks will still show up.

But preparation changes what happens next.

The unprepared panic.

The prepared respond.

Preparation does not eliminate mistakes.

It shortens recovery time.

That matters in sports.

A missed tackle is not the end if the player resets quickly.

A turnover is not the end if the team responds with composure.

A bad first half is not the end if belief remains steady.

And it matters just as much in life.

A bad meeting is not the end.
A lost opportunity is not the end.
A disappointing result is not the end.

The question is never whether adversity will arrive.

The question is whether your preparation has trained you to answer it well.

THE STANDARD OF GREATNESS

Greatness is not a moment.

It is a standard.

A standard is what you do consistently, not occasionally.

Anybody can prepare hard once in a while.

Anybody can lock in for a short season.

Anybody can be disciplined when they feel motivated.

But standards are different.

Standards do not depend on mood.

Standards do not wait on pressure.

Standards shape behavior before the moment arrives.

So what is your standard?

Do you prepare only when you feel like it?

Do you work only when people are watching?

Do you rely on motivation, or do you rely on discipline?

Standards create consistency.
Consistency builds trust.
Trust produces performance.

That is true for athletes.
That is true for teams.
That is true for coaches, leaders, business owners, parents, and anybody trying to build something meaningful.

If you want greatness, you cannot just chase big moments.

You have to build a standard strong enough to sustain them.

APPLICATION FOR ATHLETES AND FOR LIFE

For athletes, this means every rep matters.

Practice like it counts because it does.

Train under pressure.
Develop routines.

Work on weaknesses.
Stop waiting for game day to become focused.

For life and business, the same principle applies.

Prepare beyond expectations.

Build disciplined habits.
Rehearse the hard conversations.
Show up with clarity.
Stop relying on motivation and start relying on standards.

Ask yourself:

Where am I cutting corners?
Am I preparing for comfort or pressure?
Can I truly trust my preparation?

Those questions matter because pressure always tells the truth.

COACH P PROMOTION / INTEGRATION

If this chapter is challenging you, that is exactly why we do what we do.

At Inspirational University, we do not just talk about mental toughness.

We train it.

Through our Mental Performance Series, our Success Bundle courses, our weekly podcast, and our daily Words of Encouragement, we help athletes, coaches, leaders, and high performers build the mindset to move forward under pressure.

Because talent is not enough.
Potential is not enough.
You need preparation.
You need discipline.
You need a standard.

That is what mental performance training is all about.

CLOSING

When the moment comes—and it will come—you will not have time to think your way into confidence.

You will fall back on what you have prepared for.

So ask yourself:

Did I do enough?
Did I prepare with purpose?
Can I trust my work?

Because if you can trust your preparation, you will step into pressure with confidence.
You will perform with clarity.
You will recover faster from adversity.
You will move forward while others freeze.

This is Coach P.

And remember:

Mental Toughness is the ability to MOVE FORWARD under pressure.

And that starts with trusting your preparation.

CHAPTER 11

The Cost of Excellence

Coach P Signature Full Recording Script

Everybody wants to be great.

Everybody wants to win.
Everybody wants the result.
Everybody wants to be respected.
Everybody wants people to see the finish line.

But very few people ever sit down and ask the real question.

Am I willing to pay for it?

Because excellence is not free.

It never has been.
It never will be.

And that is where the separation starts.

See, a lot of people love the idea of greatness. They love the image of success. They love the applause, the recognition, the title, the scholarship, the promotion, the platform, the opportunity. They love the conversation around excellence. They love to say they want more. They love to post about discipline, about standards, about growth, about becoming elite.

But when it comes time to pay the cost, everything changes.

Because excellence is expensive.

Not expensive in money.
Expensive in discipline.
Expensive in sacrifice.
Expensive in consistency.
Expensive in mindset.
Expensive in what it demands from you when nobody is watching and when nobody is clapping.

So today, that is what we are talking about.

We are talking about the cost of excellence.

What it really requires.
Why most people never reach it.
And why the people who do reach it are not always the most talented people in the room, but they are almost always the ones most willing to keep paying the price.

This is Chapter 11.
This is your next level conversation.
And this is one of those messages that hits athletes, coaches, leaders, business people, parents, and anybody who says they want to become more than average.

Because in the end, you do not get what you say you want.

You get what you are willing to pay for.

SEGMENT 1: WHAT THE COST REALLY IS

When I say the cost of excellence, I am not talking about money.

I am talking about what excellence asks from you every day.

It asks for your time.
It asks for your focus.
It asks for your standards.
It asks for your energy.

It asks for your willingness to do what is necessary, even when it is inconvenient.

For athletes, the cost of excellence is showing up early, staying late, doing the extra rep, running through the finish line, listening to coaching, studying film, taking care of your body, controlling your emotions, and staying disciplined when distractions are everywhere.

For adults in life and business, the cost of excellence is just as real.

It is the discipline to prepare when nobody sees it.
It is the ability to keep showing up when the results are not immediate.
It is making the hard call instead of the easy one.
It is having standards when shortcuts are available.
It is staying focused when comfort is trying to pull you backward.

That is the thing about excellence. It always costs more than average is willing to pay.

Average wants convenience.
Excellence requires commitment.

Average wants quick results.
Excellence requires patience.

Average wants to feel good first.
Excellence says do the work first.

And that is why so many people stay stuck in the middle. Not because they do not have potential, but because they never accept what the process really costs.

There is always a payment attached to becoming your best.

The question is not whether the cost exists.
The question is whether you will keep paying it when the excitement wears off.

SEGMENT 2: EVERYBODY LOVES THE REWARD, FEW LOVE THE PROCESS

This is one of the hardest truths to accept.

Everybody loves the reward.

Everybody loves game day.
Everybody loves the win.
Everybody loves the spotlight.
Everybody loves the promotion.
Everybody loves the outcome when it finally shows up.

But the process?
That is where people disappear.

The process is quiet.
The process is repetitive.
The process is demanding.
The process does not always give immediate feedback.

And because of that, people start looking for shortcuts.

They want to skip steps.
They want to get results without habits.
They want to be noticed without being disciplined.
They want confidence without preparation.
They want excellence without the cost.

But that is not how this works.

There is no shortcut to becoming trustworthy under pressure.
There is no shortcut to becoming a reliable performer.
There is no shortcut to building a championship mindset.

You cannot talk your way into excellence.
You have to train your way into it.

And that means accepting that the boring parts matter.
The hidden parts matter.
The repeated parts matter.
The days when you do not feel like it matter.

The real work of excellence almost never looks glamorous.

It looks like daily discipline.
It looks like consistency.
It looks like choosing standards over feelings.

That is why so many people start strong and fade.
They were in love with the reward, but not committed to the process.

SEGMENT 3: LOCKER ROOM STORY — SAME TALENT, DIFFERENT COST

I have seen this play out so many times in athletics.

Two players.
Same age.
Same program.
Sometimes even the same amount of natural ability.

One talks a great game.
The other quietly pays the price.

One wants to be seen as a leader.
The other chooses to live like one.

One wants the starting job.
The other trains like he already understands what that job costs.

One does enough to stay around.
The other does extra because he knows enough is never enough if excellence is the standard.

Then the season comes.
Pressure comes.

Adversity comes.
Competition gets real.

And suddenly, the gap shows up.

It is not magic.
It is not luck.
It is the accumulated result of what each one paid for day after day.

I remember players who had all the physical tools, all the upside, all the athletic ability in the world. But they kept looking for ways around the process. They wanted the jersey, but not the discipline. They wanted the praise, but not the habits. They wanted the spotlight, but not the sacrifice.

Then I remember other players who maybe were not the flashiest on day one, but they kept paying. They kept listening. They kept growing. They kept training. They kept showing up with the same attitude, the same focus, and the same hunger.

And when the moment came, guess who was ready?

Not always the one with the biggest mouth.
Not always the one with the most hype.
Usually the one who paid the cost.

That is one of the greatest lessons sports teaches us.

You do not rise because you said you wanted it.
You rise because your habits proved you were willing to pay for it.

SEGMENT 4: THE FOUR PRICES OF EXCELLENCE

Let me break this down in a simple way.

If you want excellence, there are at least four prices you are going to have to pay over and over again.

The first price is discipline.

Discipline means doing what is required whether you feel like it or not.
It means your standards do not change because your emotions changed.
It means you do not need to be hyped up every day to do your job.
It means you understand that feelings are real, but they do not get the final vote.

The second price is sacrifice.

You cannot have excellence and keep every comfort.
Something always has to go.
Maybe it is wasted time.
Maybe it is distraction.
Maybe it is a bad habit.
Maybe it is being around people who keep pulling you backward.
Maybe it is your addiction to ease.

Excellence always asks: what are you willing to give up in order to become who you say you want to be?

The third price is consistency.

Anybody can do the right thing once.
Anybody can have one good day.
Anybody can be locked in when they are excited.

But can you do it again?
Can you do it tomorrow?
Can you do it when it is boring?
Can you do it when progress feels slow?
Can you do it when there is no applause attached to it?

That is where real growth happens.
Consistency turns effort into identity.

The fourth price is mental toughness.

Because all the discipline and sacrifice in the world will eventually get tested by pressure, adversity, and doubt.
And when that test comes, your mind has to be strong enough to keep you moving.

That is why I talk so much about mental performance.
That is why our work centers on mindset.
That is why the phrase matters so much: mental toughness is the ability to move forward under pressure.

Because if your mind collapses, your talent does not save you.
Your potential does not save you.
Your intentions do not save you.

Mental toughness is what allows you to keep paying the price when life gets hard.

SEGMENT 5: WHY MOST PEOPLE DO NOT PAY IT

Now let us get honest.

Why do most people stop short of excellence?

It is not because excellence is impossible.
It is because the cost keeps confronting their comfort.

Some people want comfort more than growth.

They say they want more, but they also want easy.
They want a championship standard with average-level discipline.
They want elite results while protecting every excuse.

That does not work.

Some people want instant results.

They will work for a week, maybe two, maybe a month. But if the return does not show up fast enough, they lose patience. They stop trusting the process. They start questioning whether the work matters.

But excellence is not microwave growth.
It is built slowly.
It is built layer by layer.
It is built in ways that are often invisible before they are visible.

Some people compare instead of commit.

They spend too much time looking sideways.
They watch somebody else's timeline.
They measure themselves against everybody else.
They get distracted by appearances.
They get discouraged because somebody else looks farther ahead.

Comparison drains your energy.
Commitment builds your future.

And some people quit when it gets hard.

That is the biggest separator of all.

Because it will get hard.
You will hit fatigue.
You will hit doubt.
You will hit setbacks.
You will hit moments where you wonder if the price is worth it.

And in those moments, people reveal what they really value.

The people who become excellent are not the people who never felt the weight.
They are the people who kept carrying it.

SEGMENT 6: LIFE AND BUSINESS — THE COST SHOWS UP EVERYWHERE

This conversation is not just for athletes.

This is about life.

You want to lead at a high level?
There is a cost.

You want to build a healthy family culture?
There is a cost.

You want to build something meaningful in business?
There is a cost.

You want to separate yourself from average in your profession?
There is a cost.

That cost might look like preparation.
It might look like saying no.
It might look like having hard conversations.
It might look like staying steady when others are emotional.
It might look like being dependable when others are inconsistent.
It might look like making the disciplined decision over the popular one.

The marketplace rewards value.
Leadership rewards steadiness.
Trust is built through consistency.
And all of that comes back to the same truth: excellence costs something.

In life and business, I have seen people sabotage themselves because they wanted the image of success but not the demands of success. They wanted to be respected, but they were not dependable. They wanted influence, but they were not disciplined. They wanted growth, but they would not accept correction. They wanted opportunity, but they had not prepared themselves to handle it.

That is why average keeps showing up in different clothes.

It is not always obvious.
Sometimes average looks busy.
Sometimes average sounds confident.
Sometimes average is talented.

But average still reveals itself in one place: it does not keep paying the cost.

Excellence does.

SEGMENT 7: THE COST OF AVERAGE IS HIGHER

Here is a statement I want you to sit with.

The cost of excellence is high.
But the cost of average is higher.

Average costs you your potential.
Average costs you missed opportunities.
Average costs you growth.
Average costs you trust.
Average costs you the life you could have built if you had been willing to stay disciplined longer.

A lot of people think they are protecting themselves by choosing the easier path.
What they are really doing is paying a different kind of price.

The price of regret.
The price of underachievement.
The price of knowing deep down that they left something on the table.

And that is a heavy price.

Because one day you wake up and realize you were not denied excellence.
You drifted away from it.

Not because you did not want it.
But because you stopped paying.

That is why this conversation matters.

I want people to understand that avoiding discomfort is not free.
Avoiding discipline is not free.
Avoiding standards is not free.

There is always a cost.
So you might as well choose the cost that builds something.

Choose the cost that moves you forward.
Choose the cost that strengthens you.
Choose the cost that creates a better future.

SEGMENT 8: RESOURCES THAT HELP YOU BUILD IT

This is exactly why I have built so much of my work around mental performance, discipline, and growth.

Because people do not just need inspiration.
They need training.
They need structure.
They need language for the battle they are in.
They need tools they can actually apply.

That is why I wrote Mental Toughness by Coach P.
That book is about building the mindset, discipline, and resilience to keep moving when life gets hard.

That is why we have the Mental Performance Series.
Volume 1, Passion, Belief, Achievement, is designed to help people strengthen the internal foundation that supports long-term growth.

That is why we created the Success Bundle courses.

Passion: Finding Your Dream Job.
Goal Setting: Achieve All Your Dreams.
Mindset: Moving Forward Under Pressure.

Those courses are built to help people take action, get clarity, and train the mind to operate at a higher level.

And that is also why we offer the free booklet, The Power of the Inner Game.

Because if your inner game is weak, pressure will expose it.
But if your inner game is trained, pressure can become the place where your strength shows up.

If this chapter is challenging you, do not just nod at it and move on.
Take action.
Build structure around your growth.
Get resources that help you stay in the fight.

You can find all of that at InspiringThem dot com.

SEGMENT 9: REFLECTION AND CHALLENGE

Let me slow this down and make it personal.

Where in your life are you saying you want excellence, but you are resisting the cost?

Where are you protecting comfort?
Where are you hoping for results you have not truly prepared for?
Where are you inconsistent?
Where are you asking for more while still living by average-level standards?

That is not condemnation.
That is clarity.

Because you cannot change what you refuse to confront.

And the people who grow are the people willing to tell themselves the truth.

Maybe your next level is going to require a new schedule.
Maybe it is going to require letting go of excuses.
Maybe it is going to require discipline with your time.
Maybe it is going to require emotional control.
Maybe it is going to require a tougher standard for how you prepare, how you communicate, or how you show up when things do not go your way.

Whatever it is, be honest about it.

Excellence begins to rise the moment excuses lose their voice.

And remember this: you do not need to become everything overnight.
You just need to become serious about paying today's price today.

That is how great things are built.
One payment.
One decision.
One disciplined day at a time.

CLOSING

Let me leave you with this.

Excellence is not an accident.
It is not random.
It is not reserved for a chosen few.

It is available to the people willing to pay for it.

Not once.
Not when it is convenient.
Not just when they are motivated.

Every day.

That is the cost.
That is the standard.
That is the separation.

So if you say you want more, ask yourself a better question.

Am I willing to pay for more?

Because at the end of the day, you do not get what you talk about.
You do not get what you post about.
You do not get what you wish for.

You get what you build.
You get what you repeat.
You get what you keep paying for.

And that is why excellence belongs to the disciplined.
It belongs to the committed.
It belongs to the mentally tough.
It belongs to the people who keep moving forward under pressure.

That is the message.

This is Coach P.

Keep building.
Keep growing.
Keep paying the price.

And never forget:

Mental toughness is the ability to move forward under pressure.

Excellence belongs to the ones who keep showing up and paying the cost.

CHAPTER 12

Built for the Climb

OPENING – PAUSE, CONTROLLED DELIVERY

What if the pressure you're feeling right now...

is not here to break you...

but to build you?

(Pause)

Think about that.

Because most people—

they want the top.

They want the success.

They want the recognition.

They want the results.

But they don't want the climb.

They don't want the mornings when it's hard to get up.

They don't want the days when nothing seems to be working.

They don't want the moments when doubt creeps in.

But that...

that's exactly where greatness is built.

And that's why this message matters today—

You were built for the climb.

THE REALITY OF THE CLIMB (SLOW, INTENTIONAL)

The climb is not comfortable.

It's not easy.

It's not predictable.

And it's definitely not fair.

In the locker room...

it's the player who stays after practice while everyone else leaves.

It's the one fighting for reps, fighting for recognition.

It's getting beat...

and choosing to line up again.

It's being overlooked...

and still showing up.

(Pause)

In life...

it's rejection.

It's starting over.

It's putting in effort and not seeing results right away.

And here's the truth—

The climb doesn't break people.

It reveals them.

DEEP LOCKER ROOM STORY

I remember a moment...

Locker room was quiet after a tough loss.

One player sat there—still in his gear.

Didn't say a word.

Didn't look at anyone.

Just sat there.

You could see it...

Frustration.

Doubt.

Questioning everything.

And I walked over and asked him—

"What are you going to do with this?"

(Pause)

Because that's the moment that matters.

Not the game.

Not the scoreboard.

But the response.

That player had a choice—

Let that moment define him...

or let it develop him.

And he chose to develop.

The next week?

He showed up different.

More focused.

More disciplined.

More locked in.

And over time...

he became someone others depended on.

Not because of talent—

but because of how he handled the climb.

LIFE STORY – DEEP EMOTIONAL LAYER

Now let's take that same moment into life.

Because we all have them.

Moments where things don't go your way.

Moments where you question your direction.

Moments where it feels like everything is working against you.

(Pause)

And nobody sees it.

Nobody understands the pressure.

Nobody understands the weight you're carrying.

But here's what you need to understand—

Those moments are shaping you.

They are building something inside you that success alone never could.

Resilience.

Patience.

Mental toughness.

LEADERSHIP / BUSINESS STORY LAYER

And if you're leading...

this matters even more.

Because leaders don't get to choose when things get hard.

They get tested.

Daily.

In decisions.

In pressure.

In uncertainty.

And the best leaders?

They don't run from the climb.

They embrace it.

They stay steady when others panic.

They stay focused when others get distracted.

They stay committed when others quit.

(Pause)

That's what separates leaders from everyone else.

MENTAL TOUGHNESS BREAKDOWN (EXPANDED)

Mental toughness is built through repetition.

Not just physical repetition—

but mental repetition.

Choosing discipline over emotion.

Choosing consistency over comfort.

Choosing growth over excuses.

Every day you show up...

you are either reinforcing strength—

or reinforcing weakness.

And that's a choice.

PROCESS OVER OUTCOME (EXPANDED)

Too many people are outcome-driven.

They want results now.

They want validation now.

They want success now.

But the climb doesn't reward impatience.

It rewards consistency.

It rewards discipline.

It rewards people who stay committed when it's hard.

(Pause)

Because the climb is preparing you...

for something bigger.

BOOK + COURSE INTEGRATION (NATURAL FLOW)

And this is exactly why everything we teach—

whether it's in the book

"Mental Toughness by Coach P"

or in the Mental Performance Series—

or inside our Success Bundle courses—

it all comes back to this principle:

You have to train your mind...

to handle the climb.

Because if your mind is weak—

the pressure will break you.

But if your mind is strong—

the pressure will build you.

And that's what we're focused on.

Building strength that lasts.

REFLECTION SECTION (DEEP)

So take a moment—

and be honest with yourself.

Where in your life are you avoiding the climb?

Where are you looking for shortcuts?

Where are you letting frustration slow you down?

(Pause)

Now flip it—

Where do you need to lean in?

Where do you need to show up stronger?

Where do you need to commit—fully—to the process?

FINAL BUILD (STRONG, RISING ENERGY)

Because here's the truth—

The climb is not your obstacle.

It's your opportunity.

It's your proving ground.

It's where you become who you're meant to be.

Anyone can talk about success.

Anyone can want success.

But not everyone is willing to earn it.

CLOSING

The climb builds discipline.

The climb builds identity.

The climb builds strength.

So when it gets hard—

Good.

That means you're in the right place.

(Pause)

Because you weren't made for easy.

You weren't made for comfort.

You were built for something more.

FINAL LINE (PAUSE BETWEEN EACH LINE)

You weren't made for comfort...

You were built for growth...

You were built for pressure..

You were BUILT...

FOR THE CLIMB.

ABOUT THE AUTHOR

Coach P (Jim Pusateri)

Jim Pusateri, known to many as **Coach P**, is a coach, speaker, educator, author, and creator of the *Mental Performance Series*. For decades, he has dedicated his life to helping athletes, students, teams, and everyday people develop the mindset, discipline, and resilience needed to perform at a higher level in sports and life.

Through coaching, leadership development, and mental performance training, Coach P has impacted individuals by teaching the principles of mental toughness, emotional control, confidence, leadership, and perseverance. His message is built around one core belief:

Success begins in the mind.

Coach P is also the host of the *Mental Toughness by Coach P* podcast, where he delivers weekly lessons focused on performing under pressure, building confidence, overcoming adversity, and developing the habits required for lasting success.

As the founder of <u>Inspirational University</u>, Coach P continues to provide books, courses, videos, and training resources designed to help people strengthen their mindset and unlock their potential.

His work blends lessons from athletics, leadership, business, and life into practical strategies that inspire growth both on and off the field.

Coach P believes that greatness is not reserved for a select few—it is built daily through discipline, preparation, and the willingness to keep moving forward when life gets difficult.

Train Your Mind. Elevate Your Game. Dominate Your Life.